Original title:
Palm Tree Paradise

Copyright © 2025 Creative Arts Management OÜ
All rights reserved.

Author: Harrison Blake
ISBN HARDBACK: 978-1-80581-533-4
ISBN PAPERBACK: 978-1-80581-060-5
ISBN EBOOK: 978-1-80581-533-4

Echoes of the Caribbean

In a land where coconuts dance,
Laughter swirls in the sun's glance.
Swaying hips, it's quite the scene,
A parrot thinks he reigns as king.

Beneath the skies of azure hue,
Locals joking, 'We're like the glue!'
In hammocks strung, they take a nap,
While fishies tease with a splashy clap.

Ethereal Greens and azure Seas

Minty leaves all fresh and bright,
Lizards sunbathe, what a sight!
They argue over snacks to take,
While tourists gawk at their own mistake.

On sandy shores, a crab does waltz,
Claiming territory, it never halts.
With every wave, a splash of glee,
As seashells laugh in harmony.

Under the Canopy's Protection

Beneath the shade, a feast awaits,
Tacos fly, oh what fun plates!
With salsa dancing down the trail,
And guacamole without fail.

Squirrels plot their sneaky schemes,
While tourists dive into their dreams.
Laughing loudly, they forget the sun,
In the jungle where all's just fun.

Solace Amongst the Waves

Surfboards floating like big ducks,
Waves crash with playful, funny luck.
A seagull steals someone's cold drink,
As swimmers only ponder and think.

Sunburns grinning, red like a fire,
"Next time," they chuckle, "we'll apply higher!"
With each splash, a fresh new joke,
As laughter rides on the breeze, bespoke.

Sanctuary of the Sun

Under wide hats and chasing shade,
Laughing children come to play.
Coconuts roll like soccer balls,
While seagulls steal the snacks away.

Sunscreen slips, a slippery mess,
Fried chicken, ah, what a jest!
The sunburnt dad drops his drink,
Now it's a sandcastle contest!

A Dance of Shadows

Oh, those shadows, long and lean,
Tap dancing under the bright sheen.
Scooter wheels on glittering sand,
Did you see that tumble? Oh, man!

Flip-flops fly, a stylish fling,
As beach balls bounce and seagulls sing.
A race to chase the shadow's trail,
But watch your toes, they'll make you wail!

Swaying Sentinels of the Shore

Guardians sway with calm delight,
Watching surfers wipe out in flight.
Bikini top caught in the breeze,
Time for giggles and sandy knees.

They witness lovebirds in the sun,
Sipping drinks, oh, what fun!
But watch your drink, my tipsy friend,
The tide's a sneak, it mocks the end!

Haven of the Heat

Ice cream trucks go down the street,
Melting treasures, summer's treat.
Frisbees soaring, laughter loud,
A friendly kraken wears a shroud.

Chasing shadows, slipping slides,
Somewhere, a pet crab glides and glides.
In this haven, life feels sweet,
But beware the ants at your feet!

Solace in Swaying Shadows

In a place where coconuts laugh out loud,
A squirrel wears shades, looking oh so proud.
Breezes dance, teasing my floppy hat,
The crabs hold meetings, discussing where they sat.

Lemonade spills, giggles fill the air,
As seagulls gather, plotting their next dare.
A toucan yells, 'This party's not a bore!'
While I chase the blender that rolled off the shore.

Laughter of the Coastal Breeze

The waves tell jokes as they crash with glee,
A fish jumps up, says, 'Look at me!'
Shells crack up, lying on the sand,
While my sunburned nose takes a silly stand.

Seagulls squawk tales, each one a delight,
Telling of beachgoers in a sunburned plight.
The crab on the grill says, 'This is my fate!'
While I search for my flip-flops, oh, isn't this great?

Secret Gardens Under the Starry Canopy

At night the fireflies put on a show,
Twinkling and winking, as if they know.
My picnic blanket turns into a zoo,
With ants in tuxedos looking for their cue.

The raccoons conspire, plotting a raid,
While I wonder how I got so waylaid.
Hot dogs in hand, I hear a loud crunch,
A raccoon now dances, joins in the lunch.

Spirals of Sunset Serenades

The sun bows out with a pie-in-the-sky,
Baked by clouds, it makes me sigh.
Birds come in choirs, singing off-key,
While I attempt to juggle, oh me, oh my!

As colors swirl, it's like a paint fight,
With blues and pinks, what a glorious sight.
The breeze tickles my toes and waves hello,
Dancing with shadows in evening's glow.

Tranquil Retreat in Shade and Light

In the breeze, hats fly like planes,
Sipping drinks with funny names.
The sun smiles down, a golden ray,
But the shade seems to shout, 'Come play!'

Flip-flops squeak, they dance on sand,
A crab scuttles by, it boasts, 'I'm grand!'
Beach balls bounce, laughter's aplenty,
Life's a riot, oh so carefree!

Gentle Lullaby of the Tropics

Coconuts drop like surprise gifts,
While seagulls swoop and make us shrift.
A nap in the sun, but who takes care?
That smell of sunscreen? Extreme wear!

The hammock swings, it gives a creak,
While monkeys chatter, oh so sleek.
Dreams of snacks, a feast so bright,
This lullaby sings through the night.

Dancers Under the Starlit Sky

Bare feet shuffle on the hot sand,
Twinkling lights, it's quite the band.
A limbo match breaks out with glee,
Who knew we'd be such sight to see?

Laughter erupts, a slip, a fall,
The moonbeam's glow is a curtain call.
Dance like no one is watching you,
But just wait till that wave crashes too!

Caress of the Saltwater Serenade

The tide teases toes, it's such a fuss,
Seagulls shout, 'You missed the bus!'
A splash here, a giggle there,
Waves wink and ask, 'Do you dare?'

Shells hold secrets of the deep,
As crabs put on a show, leaping steep.
With every tide, surprises pop,
Life's a whirl, and we can't stop!

Joy Amongst the Verdant Oasis

In a spot where coconuts drop,
And sunburnt tourists just can't stop,
Monkeys swing with a cheeky grin,
As they throw their snacks in the bin.

The breeze will tickle your nose,
While sand flies dance in curious rows,
Flip-flops stuck in the golden sand,
A real comedy by nature's hand.

Sipping drinks with little umbrellas,
We giggle at those funny fellas,
Who dive for a wave and just flop,
Making everyone burst out in a pop.

Laughter echoes through lush green leaves,
With crabs in tuxedos plotting heaves,
Oh, what a fun place to be free,
In this quirky land of jubilee!

Hidden Haven of the Ocean's Whisper

Here, the waves laugh as they crash,
Seagulls fuss over an old fish stash,
We watch as the tide plays peek-a-boo,
Making each moment feel brand new.

With sandcastles topped like a dream,
And sunscreen lotion in high esteem,
A spirited crab in a dance-off spins,
While sunbathers lose their tops in the wind.

The hammock sways, a gentle tease,
As we dodge the shade of mischievous trees,
The breeze whispers secrets of delight,
As tropical fish perform their night flight.

Oh, the fun that comes from this air,
Where life's a joke, and we've a flair,
For laughter springs from each salty spray,
While the sunset plays its light-hearted play!

Lush Dreams on a Sunny Shore

In a land where the sun wears shades,
And laughter blooms in wild parades,
A fish in a tutu swims on by,
Making waves with a sparkle in its eye.

With stylish shells as our best gear,
We strut along, no hint of fear,
A crab joins a conga line with a grin,
As our day of fun is set to begin.

The beach ball flies like a huge balloon,
While kids declare themselves king by noon,
Sunscreen fights spark hilarity's call,
As we slip and slide, attempting to sprawl.

When twilight hits, the bonfire's bright,
With marshmallows toasted to pure delight,
This humor-filled patch by the sea so grand,
Where laughter and joy go hand in hand!

Retreat of the Island Heart

In a nook where joy takes flight,
And critters play well into the night,
A parrot squawks jokes that make us laugh,
While a turtle slowly captures the path.

The drinks are strong, the smiles are wider,
As folks compete in a crab-walking slider,
Fluffy clouds make our heads feel light,
While we chase the sunset with sheer delight.

Yoga mats dance with the ocean's sway,
As we find our zen in a goofy way,
With each pose, there's laughter and glee,
In this whimsical spot where we're totally free.

The stars gather close for a gossip spree,
While waves share stories, just you and me,
In this hideaway of endless cheer,
We've found our happiness, oh so near!

Sunlit Changes in the Breeze

The sun shines bright on a crowded shore,
Sandy toes dance, who could ask for more?
A seagull swoops with a cheeky squawk,
Stealing my fries as I take a walk.

Umbrellas tilt in a colorful row,
Sipping coconut, watching surfers flow.
A crab scuttles by, wearing a shell,
Its tiny legs moving like it's in a spell.

Beach balls bounce like they don't fit in,
A toddler falls splashing, all covered in gin.
Laughter erupts as flip-flops fly,
Under the blue of a giggling sky.

Then someone yells, "The ice cream's in sight!"
We race for the truck, oh what a delight!
Melting before we can take a bite,
Life tastes sweeter in this shining light.

Verdant Dreams Above

Lush leaves sway in a joyful dance,
Chasing the breeze like it's in a trance.
Monkeys swing with their silly cheer,
Stealing my snacks, oh dear, oh dear!

Coconut smiles with a drink in hand,
A hammock floats, my escape so grand.
But wait! What's this? A lizard in shades,
Looks just like me, as fun escapades.

Sunset paints canvases of orange and pink,
While parakeets squawk, they never think.
A toucan drools on a tropical feast,
I drop my sandwich, my hunger increased!

Giggles rise with each goofy sight,
Waves crash softly, they feel just right.
In this paradise, laughter runs free,
Under the leaves with a joke or three.

Tranquil Escape Awaits

In a vibrant hut of woven dreams,
I hear the ocean's playful schemes.
A hammock sways, where worries take flight,
Cracking a coconut feels just right.

The sun dips low, night begins to tease,
Fireflies dancing in the gentle breeze.
A turtle pokes its head, sly with glee,
Says, 'I'm the speedster, just wait and see!'

Chairs flip and tumble in the sandy glow,
As I chase a breeze where the laughter flows.
A dance contest with napping iguanas,
I'll win with moves nobody can fathom!

Laughter twinkles like stars in the sky,
Moments like these make the heart fly high.
As the world slows down, we embrace the mirth,
In our hidden corner, we find our worth.

A Breath of Tropical Air

Breezes carry the scent of sweet fruit,
As I munch a snack, wearing flip-flop boots.
A parrot squawks from a nearby tree,
'Who's stealing my thunder?' It's just little me!

Sunshine spills like lemonade dreams,
While Uncle Joe casts his fishing schemes.
The fish swim away, they laugh in delight,
At the bait he offers—oh what a sight!

Dancing shadows from palm trees near,
While I attempt some moves, facing fear.
The neighbor's dog joins with leaps of grace,
Spinning around, oh what a race!

Tropical nights spark laughter and cheer,
As melodies float, inspiring the beer.
With each whispered joke of the gentle night,
This paradise shines, oh what a delight!

Enveloping Greeness

In the tropics where the coconuts fall,
Lizards race past on a wandering stroll.
Mangoes hang low, tempting the hearts,
While seagulls squawk tunes that get the fun starts.

Friends in flip-flops dance on the sand,
One trips and tumbles; isn't life grand?
Sipping on drinks with umbrellas so fine,
In this wild world where worries decline.

Island Serenity Unveiled

Laughter echoes beneath the sun's beam,
As crabs join the party, plotting a scheme.
The breeze tells secrets from ocean's delight,
While sunburnt tourists are in a bold fight.

Swaying in rhythm, the hammock holds tight,
A dad dozes off, what a comical sight!
The kids build a castle, one wave, it's gone,
But they laugh so loud, they keep sailing on.

Dreamscape of the Tropics

Dreamers drift long, under skies painted blue,
With snorkels in hand, they're quite the crew.
An octopus winks at a clam who despairs,
While beachgoers search for a volleyball pair.

The sun sets low, painting all in gold,
Sandy snacks vanish, the stories unfold.
A flip-flop flies, oh where will it land?
Just watch where it goes; perhaps no one planned!

Sun-Soaked Horizons

On the soft shores where sunsets ignite,
Swimmers chase waves, their giggles take flight.
A dad takes a plunge, only to find,
A crab thinking fast, leaving him blind.

As the stars twinkle, the fireflies cheer,
With marshmallows roasting, not a single fear.
Underneath palm fronds, good times unfurl,
In this quirky beach, let your laughter whirl.

Arcadia of the Orchid Winds

In a land where coconuts call,
The squirrels wear helmets, oh what a ball!
The crabs breakdance on the hot sand,
While the seagulls try to form a band.

The sun shines bright; it's a glorious sight,
As the toucans go out, ready to fight.
They argue over who's the best chef,
But all they can make is a sunburnt jest!

On floating chairs, the locals sway,
As the bananas hold a grand ballet.
Mango smoothies in hand, what a treat,
While the fish bring hummus to complement their beat.

The iguana wears glasses to read,
While the parrots gossip, with utmost speed.
In this quirky world where laughter rings,
Even the turtles are wearing bling!

Heavenly Hideaways

In a place where flip-flops reign,
The jellybeans dance in a sugar-cane chain.
Cocktails are served by lazy crabs,
While the cucumbers wear fancy blabs.

The dolphins throw a foam party, hey!
Jumping through rainbows, they laugh and play.
Under the shade of a big leaf umbrella,
Even the piña coladas are fella!

Cockatoos squawk their best bird jokes,
While the beach balls band together like folks.
They bounce and tumble in a merry dance,
Making everyone join in the silly prance.

Under the stars, the coconuts snore,
As the shore whispers tales of days lore.
In this hideaway so hilariously bright,
Live the dreams of fun, all day and night!

Horizon's Embrace

Beneath the sun, the seaweed sings,
As crabs in tuxedos plan fancy flings.
The jellyfish bring their glow on the shore,
While the seashells ticket for the dance floor.

The horizon blushes at the sunset's tease,
As flamingos try practicing their freeze.
Tide pools become little dance halls,
With sand dollars tossing their blingy balls.

In this realm of giggles and glee,
The earthworms groove with utmost spree.
Quirky creatures from far and wide,
Join together in a joyous ride.

Sun-tanned buddies sip coconut cream,
Chasing dreams like a caramel beam.
In the embrace of a horizon so bright,
Life becomes one continuous delight!

The Dance of the Winds

The breezes swirl into a graceful twirl,
While the octopus teaches a wiggly whirl.
Twisting in rhythm, the sea grass sways,
As the hermit crabs march in funky displays.

A turtle spins atop an old surfboard,
In this comedy of joy, laughter is stored.
As jellybeans popcorn with zestful glee,
The waves clap as if they're meant to be free.

Fluttering flags wave like they own the show,
While the shady palms put on a glow.
The seagulls throw confetti made of shells,
As sailors share tales of their oceanic spells.

In this dance of whispers and breezy plays,
Even the sunlight gets lost in the rays.
So come one, come all, to this whimsical spree,
Where every chuckle is a ticket to glee!

A Symphony in Green and Blue

In a land where the coconuts sway,
The dancing ducks think it's okay.
They twirl on the sand, just like pros,
While gulls in tuxedos strike silly poses.

The breeze sings a tune, oh so bright,
As crabs play poker by the moonlight.
A turtle joins in, wearing a hat,
Sipping a smoothie, imagine that!

Laughter echoes from the shore,
Where seagulls play cards and always score.
With waves that crash in joyful glee,
Who knew the sea could throw a spree?

So take a seat beneath this view,
And watch as nature jigs and skews.
It's a symphony of giggles, you see,
In this land where all feel free!

Peace Under the Whispering Canopy

Under the leaves, a hammock swings,
As monkeys plot their next wild flings.
A parrot squawks, quite the chatter,
While ants conspire about what's the matter.

The sun peeks through in a golden ray,
Why do we work? Let's just play!
A crab with shades looks quite the part,
As beach balls fly, oh, what an art!

People lounge with drinks so bright,
While toucans drop snacks, oh what a sight!
A barbecue sizzling, the aroma so fine,
"Who stole my burger?" says a cat so divine!

Laughter bubbles, spirits are high,
In this merry world, we're all a bit spry.
So kick off your shoes, let worries flee,
Find peace here, just you and me!

Whispers of the Tropics

In tropical breezes, whispers depart,
As frogs wear sunglasses, each plays their part.
A lizard does yoga, trying to pose,
While snails take notes—I suppose!

The sun winks down, a cheeky friend,
Inventing new trends, it will not end.
With drinks that fizz and fruits so bold,
The locals smile, stories unfold.

A crab on a surfboard rides the wave,
Giving high-fives, oh so brave!
While seagulls drop in for a snack and a laugh,
Playing charades, oh, what a gaffe!

So join the fun in this lively scene,
Where nature's humor reigns supreme.
In the whispers of the tropics, find your song,
Where laughter blooms and nothing's wrong!

Sunlit Canopies

Under bright canopies, the fun begins,
With squirrels doing flips, oh, for the sins!
Beneath the shade, grasshoppers hop,
While a chicken waiter takes a quick stop.

A market of colors, fruits piled high,
With laughter like bubbles floating on by.
Lemons roll races, the crowd does cheer,
As toucans judge, holding a beer.

In shady lounges, stories collide,
A hula contest where no one can hide.
With sock-clad feet dancing on warm sand,
Even the dolphins swim hand in hand!

So grab a mate, grab a drink, feel the beat,
In this sunny haven, joy is replete.
Under sunlit canopies, life gives a wink,
Join the spectacle—just don't overthink!

Elegance Amongst Emerald Leaves

In the breeze they dance and sway,
Balancing like it's ballet.
With coconuts as their best hats,
They gossip with the cheeky bats.

Underneath the bright blue skies,
They hold their heads with much surprise.
When squirrels slide and branches creak,
These leafy giants just can't speak.

The sun sets low, a grand display,
As nature sings a funny play.
In this paradise of green delight,
Even the shadows laugh at night.

So let us grin, for life is sweet,
With emerald leaves and sandy feet.
In this world, the humor thrives,
In every rustle, nature jives.

Rhythm of the Coastal Canopy

Leaves perform in grand parade,
With laughter in each leafy shade.
The crabs dance to a cheeky beat,
While geckos laugh at shuffling feet.

On sunny days, it's such a show,
As toucans honk and breezes blow.
The ocean waves join in the fun,
A symphony of sun and run.

Wacky birds in bright array,
Seem to mock the surfers' play.
With flip-flops flying in the air,
And sunburnt noses, unaware!

So come and join the coastal jive,
Where nature's humor comes alive.
In this rhythm, joy we'll glean,
Beneath the leaves, a comic scene.

Embrace of the Island's Embrace

Huggable palms in warm embrace,
Caress the air, a gentle grace.
With trunks so tall, they seem to smile,
Inviting all to stay awhile.

The coconuts roll, quite the show,
As if they're putting on a blow.
A monkey swings, a funny feat,
With laughter echoing so sweet.

The waves come in with a playful splash,
Tickling toes in a joyful crash.
With sunburned laughs and playful brawl,
The island's charm enchants us all.

So let us jump and let hearts twirl,
In this embrace, our dreams unfurl.
With every giggle, merry ways,
In this paradise, we find our play.

Lush Serenity at Dusk

As dusk wraps round with a gentle hug,
The leaves tell tales with a playful shrug.
The frogs croak jokes in the fading light,
With laughter echoing through the night.

Fireflies dance in a twinkling spree,
While flip-flops squeak with glee and glee.
The moon peeks through, a cheeky grin,
As night takes hold, let fun begin!

Waves whisper secrets to the shore,
With every roar, they ask for more.
The breeze brings news of funny sights,
As sleepy stars share silly nights.

So let us cherish this twilight cheer,
Where laughter blooms without a fear.
In the lush serenity after grace,
We find our joy, in nature's embrace.

Retreat to the Tropics

In a hammock swinging high,
An insect buzzes by.
I swat and miss with flair,
It giggles, fills the air.

Coconuts fall with a thud,
A splash in the nearby mud.
The locals laugh and shout,
'We'll drink it all, no doubt!'

Seagulls dive and steal my fries,
I can't believe my eyes!
They squawk and flap around,
While I just sit, spellbound.

Feet in sand, I grin so wide,
What a nonsensical ride!
With every silly play,
I think I'll never stray.

Breezing Through Tranquility

Life's a nap in the sun,
But then my hat did run!
A gust picked it right up,
Now it's a bird's new cup.

Drinks on ice, it's so neat,
But the ice just won't keep.
Spilling some on my toe,
And laughing like a show.

Swimsuit's way too tight,
Oh, what a squeezing sight!
I wave and tumble down,
While onlookers all frown.

But in this playful place,
I embrace the wild race.
With giggles as my guide,
I bounce along with pride.

Island Dreams Emerging

On this beach, the vibe is grand,
With shells and soft white sand.
A crab scuttles, oh so fast,
Out of my foot's pure blast.

Sunset's painting the sky bright,
I trip over, clutching tight.
A splash! I get soaked anew,
As my drink gets in the stew.

In the shops, I try to barter,
For a hat, not a starter.
The vendor laughs, I just smile,
As we dance for a while.

This island, pure delight,
With funny mishaps in sight.
I embrace all the charms,
That keep me in their arms.

The Horizon's Glow

As the sun dips down low,
All the laughter starts to grow.
A conga line forms the thrill,
With a coconut, I spill!

Oh dear, my legs are tied,
With a beach ball by my side.
I bounce and fly with glee,
While the crowd just loves me!

Fireworks pop in the night,
With colors, what a sight!
I dance with a silly flair,
Swirling sand in the air.

This paradise makes me grin,
Through blunders, let the fun begin.
With every chuckle and cheer,
I toast my fun-filled year.

Echoes of Island Life

In the shade, a coconut falls,
Cheeky crabs dance at the calls.
The sun is hot, but so is my drink,
Laughter bubbles, more fun than you think.

Seagulls squawk, they steal my fry,
They mock my sunburn, oh me, oh my!
With each splash, a giggle's released,
In this warm, sunny, feathery feast.

Neighbors snoozing, forgetting to tan,
Their beach hats blown, oh, that's the plan!
A sandcastle wobbles, then takes a dive,
It's a storm out here — the seagulls thrive!

So here I lounge, my worries are few,
Just me, some tunes, a sky so blue.
With waves that giggle and flick out their foam,
In this lively chaos, I feel at home.

Breezy Solitude

The hammock swings, I sip what's cold,
In this quiet spot, let stories unfold.
With a snack that slipped and fell on my lap,
Oh come on, seagull! That's my snack wrap!

The breeze is a flirt, plays with my hair,
Tangles it nicely, I'm in its snare.
The sun paints a smile on this silly face,
While the sand tickles toes in this calming place.

A flip-flop's gone, it must have ran,
They're faster than me, this beach is a plan!
Shadows of laughter, from waves that peek,
Where solitude's funny and time is a cheek.

So here I chill, with a grin that's wide,
As I discover new comfort in this sunny ride.
In breezy delights and whimsical cheer,
My island escape brings fun ever near.

Sun-Kissed Palms

Sunshine's bright, and so's my laugh,
I trip on my towel, oh what a gaffe!
The ice cream drips down, it's melting fast,
Here's to summer fun, make memories last!

Tanned and toasted, like a piece of bread,
My beach ball bounces, right on my head.
The ocean's a jokester, splashing away,
It tickles my toes when I give it a play.

With sand in my hair and joy in my heart,
I build silly towers, that's just the start.
A crab walks by with a sassy mean strut,
I'm no match for that pincher in his beach hut!

So let's dance in the waves, with friends by our side,
In a sun-kissed world where laughter can't hide.
With memories bright like the midday sun,
Every moment here is pure, silly fun.

Where the Waves Draw Near

The waves whisper secrets, they've shared with the sand,
With each playful splash, they tease my hand.
I dive and I dodge, with much splish-splash flair,
But oops, now I'm soaked, what a way to beware!

Floating on air, or so I thought,
A seaweed blanket, oh, what a knot!
I giggle at fish as they dart in delight,
Who knew my adventure would take such a flight?

The sun slowly winks, painting gold on my cheeks,
While crabs have a rave, with their little squeaks.
Life's just a party, with a twist at the sea,
In this whimsical world, I'm as happy as can be.

So here on the shore, where the wild waves cheer,
I dance with the tides, feel the happiness near.
With laughter that echoes through the breeze and the foam,
Each moment a treasure, a big splash of home.

Whispers of the Tropical Breeze

In the shadow of a coconut's grin,
The breeze tells jokes, where laughs begin.
Laughter floats on the waves so free,
Even the fish are laughing with glee.

A seagull danced, to my surprise,
With sunglasses on, what a funny guise!
He cawed a tune, a catchy tune,
Making waves with jokes under the moon.

Tropical fruits giggle in their bowls,
Bananas tell tales, while mangoes roll.
The sun is a comedian, no need for a show,
In this paradise, laughter steals the glow.

So grab your drinks and kick off your shoes,
Join in the laughter, there's nothing to lose.
With flip-flops a-flapping, we'll dance with ease,
In the whispers of the tropical breeze.

Shadows Beneath the Swaying Fronds

Underneath the leafy hats that sway,
Laughter hides in shadows, come out and play.
A iguana grins, he's a sly little guy,
In this leafy lounge, no need to be shy.

The crabs hold hands, they've formed a band,
Playing tiny drums on the warm, golden sand.
Turtles shuffle, moving slow and slick,
While the octopus juggles, what a funny trick!

Coconuts gossip; they're the local news,
Spilling the beans on the funniest crews.
The breeze takes a jab at the sun, oh so bright,
In a showdown of giggles, it's a pure delight!

So let's grab a seat, with our drinks in tow,
Watching shadows dance, as the sun sets low.
In the antics and laughter that nature sends,
Life's a comedy, made with good friends.

Sunlit Sway of Island Dreams

The sun smiles at me with a cheeky grin,
While waves play peek-a-boo, where do they begin?
Every flip-flop sounds like a laugh track,
In this sandy playground, there's no looking back.

A parrot squawks jokes, in colors so bright,
With humor so good, it's hard to take flight.
Sunbathers chuckle, sunscreen on their nose,
Life's just a giggle, as everyone knows!

The hammock's a stage, swaying with flair,
As I dangle and giggle, without a care.
And if you should fall, in a flip or a flop,
Just roll with the laughter, never you stop!

So bask in the sun, let your worries dissolve,
In this island dream, where we all can evolve.
With every sweet giggle that sparkles in beams,
Life's a delightful, sunlit sway of dreams.

Oasis of the Sun-Soaked Haven

Nestled in the sun, where the fun never stops,
Floaties and laughter bubble over in plops.
Sunscreen machines put out giggle-filled spray,
Making every sunscreen-smeared face a display!

Fish in the coral are quite the pranksters,
Doing fishy flips, they're real twisty tanksters.
The beach ball shouts, 'I'm the best ball around!'
While waves nudge gently, with each splashy sound.

Ice cream melts faster than jokes can unfold,
Sprinkling hilarity as flavors go cold.
The sun overhead, the world naked and free,
In this oasis, we laugh heartily!

So join in the fun, with a grin ear to ear,
Let's splash in the waves, spreading joy and cheer.
In this sun-soaked haven, life's all about play,
With laughter and sunshine leading the way!

Coastal Reverie

Under the sun, my hair's a mess,
Sandy toes, oh what a dress!
Seagulls squawk, they steal my fries,
I wave goodbye with rolling eyes.

Coconut drinks that never end,
My beach ball's now my funny friend.
I dive for shells, I find my shoe,
Now that's a prize, it's got my glue!

Crabs on the shore, they dance about,
I try to join, they twist and shout.
Sunburned and smiling, I finally concede,
To the ice cream truck, oh yes indeed!

Waves keep crashing, I'm laughing hard,
Life here is quite the backyard.
I'll never leave, don't call my bluff,
In this coastal dream, I've found enough!

Tropical Dreams Unfurled

Beneath the shade, my hammock swings,
A lizard on my toe just clings.
Sipping juice, a straw misfit,
I giggle loud, oh what a hit!

The breeze brings whispers, sweet lilting calls,
As I dodge that seagull's food brawls.
Tanned and toasty like a bun,
I wonder if I'm done with fun?

In flip-flops, I daringly prance,
Almost tripped in a salsa dance.
With waves for rhythm, I shimmy and sway,
Why do I feel like a buffet?

Coconuts laughing, trees waving low,
They gossip of palapas and sunsets' glow.
But here I sit, the world's my stage,
A comedy show, I turn the page!

The Shade's Embrace

Under leaves so green and broad,
I nap and snore, give thanks to God.
A parrot squawks, my dreams go wild,
In this cozy nook, I'm just a child.

The sun's a prankster, always sneaky,
Making my ice cream feel so freaky.
I grab my hat, it flies away,
Outrunning me, what a glorious play!

Ooh, the waves tease with their splash,
Twisting my hair, oh what a mash!
I call it art, this salty hue,
Complimented by chips and a cold brew.

Here in my corner, laughter, delight,
No worries to bother, just joy in sight.
With sunburned cheeks and dreams in place,
Life's funny, so let's embrace!

Horizon of Happiness

Gazing out where sea meets sky,
A crab's my friend, oh me, oh my!
He pinches my toe, I laugh and squeal,
Together we dance like a wiggly wheel.

With sunscreen slathered, I take my stand,
Making sure the beach dogs understand.
A frisbee flies, but I just wave,
Catching my breath is what I crave.

Napping on sunbeams, warm and bright,
Dreams can take flight, like kites in sight.
The laughter here never seems to cease,
I spark the joy, a little peace!

Clouds pull tricks, they start to race,
I chase them down at a comical pace.
With waves crashing, life's a craze,
In this giggly place, I spend my days!

Embracing Coastal Dreams

Sandy toes and silly hats,
Chasing crabs and splashing spats,
Laughter echoes, bright and clear,
Who needs a chair? Just bring the beer!

Sunny days and ice cream cones,
Seagulls stealing your phone's ringtones,
Grilled fish dances on the grill,
With every bite, we're feeling ill.

The Scent of Ocean Breeze

Wafting scents of fishy fries,
Seagulls squawking, oh what a surprise!
Tanning bodies turning bright,
Flip-flops flapping, what a sight!

Spray-on tans and sandy faces,
Searching for misplaced sunrises,
Splashing waves, we lose our cares,
Until the tide steals all our chairs.

Warmth in Green Shadows

Coconuts and laughter blend,
Underneath the trees, we spend,
A monkey swings with great delight,
Stealing snacks, what a funny sight!

Sunburnt noses, topsy-turvy,
Jumping waves, feeling quite swervy,
Cool drinks served with silly straws,
All hail the beach — our topsy jaws!

Celestial Reflections by the Shore

Stars blink bright above the waves,
Mermaids splash, just like the braves,
Floating thoughts like driftwood free,
We ponder life — where's my tea?

Sandcastles rise and tumble down,
Waves wash whispers all around,
We celebrate with silly cheer,
As nightfall dances, way up here.

Verdant Bliss

In a land where coconuts fall,
The sun's a disco ball.
With flip-flops and sunscreen in tow,
Let the breezy vibe flow.

Seagulls wear shades, they strut and peck,
Building castles, what the heck!
A hammock sways, it calls my name,
Life is just a silly game.

Sipping drinks with umbrellas aflame,
While bantering with a crab named James.
His dance moves make my sides split,
Who knew a crustacean could be so hip?

Underneath the banana moon,
Trying to sing a tropical tune.
Laughter rolls like the ocean's waves,
In this paradise, we are all knaves.

Golden Sands and Green Dreams

On golden shores where laughter reigns,
Sand in my shorts, oh, what a pain!
Tidal waves, I try to outrun,
Why do they think this is fun?

The sun burns bright, my skin's a fry,
With seagulls diving from the sky.
Chase the waves, I trip and fall,
A graceful fish? Not at all.

Children digging with tiny spades,
Building kingdoms, hoping for parades.
A mermaid's tail? Just a flip-flop!
In this comedy, we can't stop!

As dusk descends, we dance and sway,
Lost in rhythm, come what may.
With friends around, the night is deep,
In this sandy dream, we'll never sleep.

The Rhythm of the Tropics

Underneath the sway of green,
A conga line, a wacky scene.
Dancing with a coconut in hand,
The funniest thing in this strange land.

Laughter echoes through the palms,
As we serenade the sunsets' balms.
Careful now, don't trip on that shell,
Who knew the ocean could cast such a spell?

Flip-flops flying left and right,
Chasing crabs that just won't fight.
A hula hoop that spins and glows,
Even the fish are in on the show!

The starry sky, a canvas bright,
We laugh until the morning light.
In a rhythm so silly and free,
Embracing all this comedy!

Lush Heights of Contentment

Climbing up the tree with a grin,
My hat flies off, oh, where've you been?
The view from here? Quite absurd,
Did I just see a flying bird?

Tropicals swaying like an old-time dance,
As I try to catch a lazy glance.
Fruits of dreams hanging so high,
I'm just a monkey, giving a try.

The breeze, it tickles; I start to wiggle,
Finding myself in a goofy jiggle.
Bananas slip from my careful grasp,
Sometimes bliss comes with a rasp.

Endless laughter fills the air,
With friends around, there's nothing to compare.
In these lush highs, I find my charm,
A paradise, silly and warm.

Nature's Contemplation

Coconuts are rolling, oh dear,
I fear they've lost their sense of cheer.
They bounce and laugh, right off the sand,
Shouting, "We're the best band in the land!"

Seagulls squawk with dubious tones,
Wondering now, just where are the cones?
A crab in shades, he takes a stroll,
Claiming the beach was his original goal.

Under sunshine, the flip-flops dance,
Each toe is prancing, what a chance!
With laughter echoing beneath the sun,
Every beach bum knows it's always fun!

The waves chime in, a rhythmic clap,
Crabs hold a party, but take a nap.
Bikini hula and sunscreen spray,
In this land of mirth, we'll always stay!

Sanctuary of Swaying Leaves

A breeze that giggles through the trees,
Telling secrets with the utmost ease.
Lizards compete in a race with flies,
While squirrels shoot acorns at the skies.

Fronds wave like hands at a grand parade,
Cheering on waves that wash and fade.
Coconuts drumming on sandy floor,
Remind us life's a wild uproar!

Umbrellas bloom like flowers bright,
Who knows which color will take flight?
Sun hats and shades, all set to sway,
As laughter echoes throughout the day.

The sun's a joker, playing peek-a-boo,
What will he do? We've not a clue!
But in this leafy, giggling seat,
Every heartbeat dances to the beat!

Secrets of the Sea Breeze

Whispers of waves against the rocks,
The sea tells tales with quite a box.
Drifting hopes on a salty wave,
A fish wears a hat, oh how it braves!

Dolphins leap with a playful grin,
Challenging gulls to a merry spin.
"Who's the king of the ocean's show?"
Each creature dances with a jazzy flow.

Seagulls strut with a sassy flair,
Hoarding snacks without a care.
The crabs join in with a sideways run,
If you're not laughing, are you having fun?

The echoes of laughter fill the air,
Even the clams lift up a chair.
In this world where whimsy grows,
Every breeze brings joy in rows!

Warmth Under the Fronds

Sunbeams sprinkle like confetti here,
Making shadows that cheer and cheer.
A pineapple dances, twirls with ease,
Beneath the fronds, it aims to please.

Chairs made of shells sing a bright tune,
As young sprouts giggle and flowers swoon.
A sunscreen bottle slips and trips,
While sunscreen-wearing fish take dips.

Flip-flops argue on who's the boss,
While sunburn jokes are worth the loss.
Banana peels plot a slippery fate,
As laughter lingers, never too late.

So here we bask, in joy and fun,
Underneath the warmth of the golden sun.
With every chuckle, our hearts expand,
This silly paradise is simply grand!

Enchanted Silhouettes

In shadows swaying, silly mates,
Dance around like tipsy plates.
A coconut falls with a splat,
'The prize!' they shout, and that's that.

Sun-kissed laughter fills the air,
Chasing waves without a care.
A crab joins in, starts to groove,
Wiggling sideways, making us move.

Seagulls squawk, and we all cheer,
As beach balls bounce, let's grab a beer!
Flip-flops flying, heads to the sky,
Splashing water, oh my, oh my!

With every sunset, our shenanigans swell,
In our quirky kingdom, we bid farewell.
We'll return for the fun that never ends,
In this paradise where laughter transcends.

Nature's Canopy of Bliss

Under fronds, we lay like logs,
Spying on the frolicking frogs.
Rum drinks spill, oh what a sight,
As monkeys yell and join the fight.

Bright sarongs dance like crazy fish,
The breeze carries a swaying wish.
Sandy feet and goofy grins,
Who needs plans when fun begins?

Beneath the sun, shenanigans start,
With quirky shells as works of art.
Jellyfish join our dance parade,
Knocking into legs, they invade!

As dusk descends, we trade our tales,
Of seagull races and silly fails.
Each moment here is pure delight,
In this wild, whimsical light.

The Language of the Breeze

Whispers float on gentle winds,
As dancing leaves make foolish spins.
The sun hides behind a cheeky cloud,
While waves applaud, a rowdy crowd.

Idiots with surfboards collide,
Splashing water, trying to glide.
A sea turtle drops by to see,
What wacky stunts are supposed to be!

Tropical drinks, with tiny hats,
Mocking us like feisty gnats.
Laughter echoes, the sky's ablaze,
In our own amusing maze.

With each gust, more giggles rise,
Mirrored in the waves' bright guise.
As time drifts on, so do we,
In nature's laugh, our spirits free!

Timeless Isles of Tranquility

Barefoot adventurers roam the shore,
Building castles—who needs more?
A seashell sticks to someone's shoe,
As if to say, "Oh, what's this goo?"

Crabs wear hats made of leafy greens,
Strutting like royalty, oh what scenes!
A sunburned penguin sells ice cream,
While tourists smile, it's like a dream.

The hammock swings with giggling flair,
As each new snack becomes a dare.
Flip-flops score points while we sneak bites,
Claiming the best, oh what delights!

As the sun dips low, we wave goodbye,
To coconut dreams and a painted sky.
In this whimsical riddle, we'll play our part,
Each moment here captures the heart.

Serenade Under the Fronds

Beneath the leafy dancers, we sing,
With coconuts chatting, oh what a thing!
The sun's a lazy cat, lounging all day,
While crabs throw a party, in their own way.

A parrot's gossip fills the humid air,
As fish wear sunglasses, like they don't care.
We sip on our drinks, with umbrellas so bright,
As sand tickles toes, what a silly sight!

The waves make us giggle, they splash and roar,
We surf on our flip-flops, who needs much more?
Oh, to live in a world where laughter runs free,
Best get a hammock, it's calling for me!

So here's to the ferns, the fun that they bring,
With each silly moment, our hearts start to sing.
For nothing like this, could ever compare,
To a serenade shared, with the island air.

Oasis of Serenity

In the shade where laughter spills and glows,
I met a wise turtle who just struck a pose.
He said, "Slow it down, life's a kooky race,
Just chill like a lizard in this cozy space."

Cacti wear hats, as they sift through the sand,
While iguanas groove, with a dance so grand.
The river's a joker, with ripples and grins,
Finding humor in whirlpools, like drinks with no sins.

We feast on the fruits that drop from above,
Each bite full of giggles, like sweet little love.
The sun tries to tickle our noses all day,
But like good comedians, we just laugh and play.

So let's raise our cups to this quirky zone,
Where breezes hold secrets and laughter's well-known.
In this oasis, every moment's a cheer,
For life's better served with some whimsy and beer!

Dancing Leaves in the Breeze

The leaves wave 'hello' with a joyous grace,
They gossip about us, in this wondrous place.
A frog strums a lute, while the sun claps along,
As we join their concert, feeling merry and strong.

The fish in the lagoon are wearing their hats,
They're bouncing to rhythms of sound, oh so fats!
Every splash is a dance move, quick on their toes,
Creating a scene that everyone knows.

As we twirl in the twilight, with cool drinks in hand,
The stars join our party, oh isn't it grand?
The crickets recite their sweet little rhymes,
While we giggle and chuckle, in our sun-kissed prime.

So let's sway with the breeze, in this dance that's our own,

In the realm where the silly and sweet are well-grown.
With songs in our hearts and joy in our feet,
We'll waltz with the leaves 'til the night's bittersweet!

Emerald Skies Above

With emerald hues splashed upon the sky,
We chuckle at clouds that just drift and fly.
A dolphin performs, with a flip and a splash,
As the sun spills its gold, oh what a flash!

Underneath this circus of turquoise and zest,
We bask in the warmth, feeling truly blessed.
A crab makes a joke, then trips on its claw,
We burst into laughter, what a humorous flaw!

The breeze tells us secrets in playful tones,
As we chase the shadows, and dance with the cones.
Life's a beachside comedy, full of delight,
So let's grab our friends, and relish the night.

For in moments like this, when the humor runs high,
We find pure joy under the vast, open sky.
With memories woven through laughter and cheer,
Here's to emerald dreams, oh let's hold them dear!

Coconut Dreams and Ocean Breezes

Coconuts dancing in the breeze,
A monkey's swinging with such ease.
He drops his fruit, oh what a mess,
And blames it on the seas, I guess!

The sand is hot, my toes are fried,
I thought I saw a crab that lied.
It claimed to be a beachside star,
But really, it's just there to spar!

Surfboards wobble, wipeouts galore,
We laugh so hard, we can't take more.
With sunburnt noses and giggled screams,
Here's to our wild coconut dreams!

An ocean breeze with humor sways,
While birds pick up on the silly ways.
In this bright land of joy and cheer,
We surf the waves and drink cold beer!

Bliss in the Tropical Canopy

Swinging high in leafy greens,
A toucan squawks with quirky scenes.
It wears a hat made out of leaves,
And all the monkeys roll their sleeves!

The sun peeks through the mottled shade,
As we play games that seem half-made.
With coconuts and laughter loud,
Pretending to be part of the crowd!

A gecko struts, its dance obscene,
While we sip drinks from bowls pristine.
A little splash, a friendly fight,
In this green hug, everything's right!

With fruity drinks and silly tunes,
We laugh beneath tropical moons.
In this bright world, we're all so free,
Embracing the bliss we can't foresee!

Luxuriating in Green Embrace

In shaded nooks by vibrant stems,
We feast like kings on fruits from gems.
A parrot squawks out secrets near,
That make us chuckle, bring the cheer!

The breeze carries a playful tease,
As lizards sneak and slip with ease.
A hammock swings, our naps delayed,
While nature hums its serenade!

We paint our faces with wild hues,
And dance with crabs to comic tunes.
In this embrace of laughter bright,
We lounge and laugh from day to night!

So here we are, just living free,
Creating moments, wild as can be.
Embracing joy in nature's space,
In the funny, green embrace we trace!

Escape Amongst the Greens

In a hammock, I swung to and fro,
Until a squirrel put on a show.
He stole my sandwich, dashed with glee,
Who knew they'd be so bold and free?

The palm leaves dance in a gentle breeze,
While I sip on a drink, attempting to tease.
But it slipped my grasp, spilled on my shoe,
The colorful mess just brightened the view!

In the shade, a breeze felt just right,
But bees buzzed in to spoil my plight.
"Partition, please!" I begged of the air,
But they surrounded; my chocolate laid bare!

Yet here I sit, I won't run away,
Each mishap just brightens my day.
With laughter echoing through the greens,
I toast to life and its silly scenes.

The Essence of Escape

In flip-flops I wander, so free and alive,
The sun hugs my shoulders, a quest to survive.
Seagulls are gossiping, making a scene,
As I chase my ice cream, like a kid on a screen.

Towels are tangled, who borrowed my shade?
And sand in my sandwich? What a charade!
But laughter ignites like the waves on the shore,
With every misstep, I'm craving for more.

A sunburnt forehead, a funny new look,
My friends can't stop chuckling, it's all in the book.
A coconut falls, with a thud and a roll,
Funny how life's little mishaps take toll.

Yet here by the shoreline, with sand in my shoe,
I dance like a fool, yes, I really do!
The essence of joy, in this goofy retreat,
In every misadventure, life's bittersweet.

Symphony of the Salty Winds

The salty breeze laughs, as it tousles my hair,
I trip on a wave like a fish in fresh air.
With sunscreen in hand, oh what a fine sight,
My buddy just ziplined, now is it day or night?

A crab walks by, with a sideways concern,
What's that in my cooler? Oh no, it's my churn!
I dance with the pelicans, let them take lead,
But step on a shell, and oh how I plead!

The sun is now setting, it's painting the sky,
I take a deep breath, let out a big sigh.
Eluding the chores, so far from the grind,
This symphony plays, to a drum I can't mind.

So here's to the laughter, the quirks we can share,
In patches of sun, let's not have a care!
The salty winds hum a tune, oh so sweet,
Reminding us all, life's small things can't be beat.

Swaying Guardians of the Coast

Those swaying sentinels, towering so high,
Guarding my drinks as the breeze passes by.
A hammock laughs softly, it knows what I crave,
And just like my nap, it's a little bit brave.

A game of beach volleyball, oh what a mess,
With flip-flops and laughter, we're all in distress.
The final shot lands in a stranger's sunblock,
And chaos erupts, oh what a great shock!

Seagulls are chirping, with sass and some flair,
As I try to sneak chips while they just stare.
Their beaks are all pointing, it's quite a display,
The guardians watch on, they seem to say "Hey!"

We stumble through games, and run in the sea,
Building sand castles, just look at me!
The sun kisses us all, with a toast from the sky,
In goofy retreats, we all say goodbye.

Whispers of the Tropic Night

As stars peep and twinkle, I feel quite alive,
The moon joins the party, oh what a surprise!
With salsa in the air, the crickets keep beat,
It's a dance of our shadows, a laughter retreat.

A lizard trots by, with moves oh so slick,
He steals my taco, now that's quite a trick!
With friends all around, we burst into song,
Who knew the beach vibes could be this strong?

The waves whisper secrets, while we sway like fools,
In the glow of the fire, forgot all the rules.
We spin and we twirl, without any care,
Under whispers of night, we breathe salty air.

So here's to the laughter, and moments we crave,
In the quirky embrace of the ocean's warm wave.
Together we'll cherish each goofy delight,
In tropical wonders, we flourish tonight.

www.ingramcontent.com/pod-product-compliance
Lightning Source LLC
Chambersburg PA
CBHW072120070526
44585CB00016B/1508